Cameos

Timeless Masterpieces of Glyptic Art

All images are from the personal collection or inventory of the publisher.

© 2017 Arthur L. Comer, Jr.

All rights reserved. No part of this book may be reproduced or transmitted in any form or by any means, electronic or mechanical, including photocopying or by any information storage and retrieval system without written permission from the publisher.

ISBN: 978 0 975 2760 1 3

Table of Contents

Preface... 3

Lava and Coral Cameos.. 4 - 10

Stone and Shell Cameos.. 11 - 57

Cameo Rings and Stickpins... 58 - 73

Cameos Made From Bakelite and Alternative Materials............... 74 - 94

Cameos, for thousands of years, have been cherished possessions of kings, queens, emperors and others with the financial means to acquire them. Today's collectors have the opportunity to preserve this rare glyptic art form for future generations. The stunning Victorian-era woman pictured above is wearing, in a traditional manner, a mesh cameo bracelet and a cameo brooch centered on the collar just below the neckline.

Preface

This second and expanded edition of Cameos - Timeless Masterpieces of Glyptic Art allows the collector a fresh look at the artistic ability of the artisans who put their sweat and tears into their creations. Unlike the mass-produced machine-made clones found in the marketplace today, each piece presented, unless otherwise noted, represents a time-consuming labor of love in its conception, hand-carving, and mounting. As stated in the first edition, it is not the author's objective to provide an in-depth study of the history of cameos or their individual values. Values of these unique works of glyptic art are the prices that a willing seller will accept and a motivated buyer is willing to pay. The reader should be mindful that each hand-carved cameo is unique, a one-of-a-kind creation. Although the images may be similar, no two stones, shells or other materials used to carve the finished works of art are identical in nature. A cameo carver requires the skills of an artist and the ability of a sculptor to bring a piece to life in a three-dimensional form. The carver must also have the technical know-how to evaluate the individual qualities of the carving material to best use its unique characteristics in the finished artwork. It takes a Master carver years to develop the expertise needed to render heirloom quality pieces. A collector will easily recognize the work of a Master carver when comparing the attention to details in the renderings of several pieces. The purpose of this pictorial reference book is to inspire the novice collector to search for the absolute best quality cameo he or she is able to afford and to provide an affordable pictorial reference for recognizing vintage and antique cameos. It is the author's hope that this reference book will enable the collector to make sound educated decisions about purchasing an individual cameo or building a meaningful collection. A quality picture can often portray what cannot be adequately expressed in the written word.

Arthur L. Comer, Jr.

<Sardonyx Shell
cassis
madagascariensis

Carnelian Shell >
cassis rufa

Lava and Coral Cameos

Idar-Oberstein, Germany has for centuries been recognized as the center for most hardstone cameo production. Although hardstone cameos predate shell cameos by centuries, today, shell cameos are more readily found in the marketplace. The ancient town of Torre del Greco, Italy, situated near Naples at the base of Mount Vesuvius, can lay claim to being the world's largest producer of shell and coral cameos. Many lava cameos were also carved there.

All other criteria being equal, hardstone cameos demand higher prices than shell cameos. Hardstone cameos are more labor-intensive and difficult to carve. With the exception of ancient cameos, condition and quality of the hand carving should be your first consideration when making a purchase. Rarity, material, and mounting are other considerations to take into account. Hand-carved shell cameos have an apparent concaved surface, are transparent, and close inspection will show visible signs of the use of carving tools. Stone or shell cameos that have been ultrasonically-made, as opposed to being hand-carved, lack undercutting (cut in relief from the background). Visible signs of carving marks <u>will not</u> be seen and they will have a fresh-fallen snow look to the surface when examined with a 10x loupe. Like their hand-carved one-of-a-kind originals, the <u>carving materials</u> used in ultrasonically mass-produced cameo clones <u>will have</u> individual characteristics, but that is where the similarities to hand-carved pieces end.

Greco-Roman Woman Brooch #1741
Size: 32mm x 25mm · Weight: 7.7 grams
Mounting: 14K Gold
Period: Mid - Late Victorian
Material: Brown-tone Lava · Carved in high relief

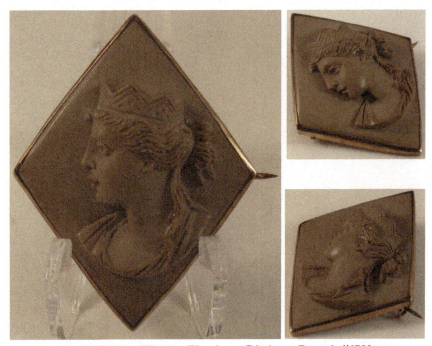

Greco-Roman Woman Wearing a Diadem · Brooch #1720
Size: 38mm x 30mm · Weight: 6.6 grams · Mounting: 9K Gold
Period: Mid - Late Victorian
Material: Brown-tone Lava · Carved in medium relief

Lava cameos are carved in a multitude of colors varying from white, gray, shades of beige, yellow, black, reddish and greenish-brown tones.

Note the tube hinge, pin that extends beyond the border of the mounting, and the "C" catch/closure. All characteristics of early Victorian-era pieces.

Greco-Roman Women Brooch #1652
Size: 32mm x 18mm
Weight: 5.5 grams
Mounting: .800 Silver
Period: Mid - Late Victorian
Material: Brown-tone Lava
Carved in medium relief

Greco-Roman Woman Brooch #1733
Size: 42mm x 34mm · Weight: 13.8 grams · Mounting: Not Mounted
Period: Mid - Late Victorian
Material: White Lava · Carved in medium relief

Bacchante Maiden Cameo Brooch #1757
A follower of Dionysus (Bacchus),
god of wine and fertility
Size: 42mm x 32mm · Weight: 16.6 grams
Mounting: Brass/Bronze
Period: Mid - Late Victorian
Material: Brown-tone Lava
Carved in high relief

St. Isidore - Farmer Patron Cameo Pendant #1754
Size: 42mm x 34mm · Weight: 13.8 grams · Mounting: Sterling Silver
Period: Mid - Late Victorian
Material: Brown-tone Lava · Carved in high relief

Isidore the Farmer, born circa 1070 in Madrid, Kingdom of Castile, was a Spanish farmworker known for his piety toward the poor and animals. He is the Catholic patron saint of farmers and of Madrid, and of La Ceiba, Honduras.

Greco-Roman Woman Cameo #1483
Size: 18mm x 13mm · Weight: 1.6 grams · Mounting: Not Mounted
Period: Mid - Late Victorian
Material: Salmon & Creamy White Coral · Carved in medium relief

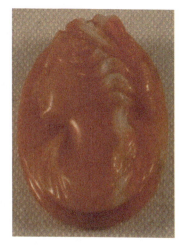

Greco-Roman Woman Brooch/Pendant & Earrings #1735
Size: (Brooch) 43mm x 33mm, (Earrings) 13mm x 11mm
Weight: (Brooch) 12.1 grams, (Earrings) 4.7 grams
Mounting: 18K Gold · Period: Mid - Late Victorian
Material: Angel Skin Coral · Carved in medium relief

Stone and Shell Cameos

When circa-dating cameos by mount and fastener types collectors should always be mindful that many vintage and antique cameos were reset in later mountings because of damage to the cameo or to the original mounting. During periods of high precious metal values many owners, not fully appreciating the artistic value of the pieces they owned, removed cameos from their gold and silver mounts and sold the metal. It is therefore not uncommon to find a cameo that is possibly hundreds of years old in a modern mounting. This makes the cameo almost, but not impossible, to accurately date. The carving material used, carving style, hairstyles, facial characteristic and other determining factors are addressed in Anna M. Miller's 4th Edition of Cameos Old & New, an excellent resource for expanding your knowledge of cameo history and identification.

White gold first appeared in the marketplace around 1920. Earlier pieces believed to be white gold, in fact, may be made of platinum. Habille cameos (cameos with a figure wearing/embedded with precious stones) came on the scene in the mid-Victorian period. The Victorian period also accounts for the majority of lava cameos. Although coral was used as early as the Renaissance period, most coral cameos now found in the marketplace are products of the Victorian period. Prior to the 15th-century, cameos were almost exclusively carved from precious and semi-precious gemstones. Since the middle to the late 1800s, because of its ease of carving as compared to gemstones and because of the multicolor layers it possesses, shell became the most used material for hand-carved cameos.

John the Baptist Brooch #1681 · Size: 73mm x 63mm
Weight: 19.6 grams · Mounting: Gilt Bronze/Brass
Period: Mid - Late Victorian
Material: Shell (Carnelian) · Carved in low relief

Greco-Roman Soldier Brooch #1451 · Size: 44mm x 30mm
Weight: 10.6 grams · Mounting: Gilt Bronze/Brass
Period: Victorian
Material: Shell (Sardonyx) · Carved in low relief

Roman Soldier Pendant/Brooch #1517 · Size: 38mm x 29mm
Weight: 7.7 grams · Mounting: .800 Silver · Period: Mid Victorian
Material: Shell (Carnelian) · Carved in low relief

3 Images Cameo Bracelet · Signed SIMMONS #1756
Each Cameo Size: 12mm x 11mm · Weight: 7.3 grams
Mounting: Rolled Gold/Gold Filled
Period: Edwardian/Art Deco
Material: Shell (Carnelian) · Carved in low relief

Greco-Roman Image
Mesh Bracelet with Tassels #1755
Size: Adjustable Length
Mesh: 8mm wide
Weight: 14.1 grams
Mounting: Rolled Gold/Gold Filled
Period: Victorian
Material: Hardstone
Cameo carved in medium relief

Mother and Daughter Cottage Scene #1475
Size: 49mm x 40mm · Weight: 9.9 grams
Mounting: Not Mounted · Period: Unknown
Material: Shell (Carnelian) · Carved in low relief

Woman at the Well Brooch #1734
Size: 46mm x 37mm · Weight: 11.8 grams
Mounting: .800 Silver
Period: Edwardian
Material: Shell (Carnelian) · Carved in low relief

Full-Figure Woman Image Locket Pendant #1419
Size: 26mm x 59mm · Weight: 14.2 grams
Mounting: Gilt Bronze/Brass · Period: Art Nouveau/Art Deco
Material: Hardstone · Carved in low relief

Greco-Roman Woman Image Brooch #1469
Size: 75mm x 24mm · Weight: 24.8 grams
Mounting: Onyx and 14K Gold · Period: Art Nouveau
Material: Hardstone (Onyx) with 8 Seed Pearls · Carved in low relief

Greco-Roman Image Mourning Brooch #1535
Size: 44mm x 47mm · Weight: 14.5 grams
Mounting: Gilt Brass/Bronze · Period: Edwardian/Art Deco
Material: Hardstone with Seed Pearl · Carved in low relief

Note the tube hinge, pin stem that does not extend beyond the mounting of the piece, and the safety catch/closure. These transitions in catch/closure styles from that of the Victorian period are characteristic of pieces made in the early Edwardian/Art Deco period.

Greek Goddess Belt Buckle #1758

This rare find massive belt buckle is a well-carved cameo and believed to depict the Muse of Erotic Poetry, Erato, a goddess associated with Apollo. Erato is often represented playing a lyre.

Weight: 60.1 grams · Size: 79mm x 70mm
Mounting: Pinchbeck/Gilt Brass
Period: Early - Mid Victorian
Material: Shell (Carnelian) · Carved in low/medium relief

Greco-Roman Image Bracelet #1576
Size: 8mm (Bottom of Band) x 22mm (Cameo Height) · Weight: 21.6 grams
Mounting: Gold-filled Signed "W&SB" · Period: Edwardian/Art Deco
Material: Shell (Angel Skin) · Carved in low relief

Greco-Roman Soldier Cuff Links #1684
Size: 17mm x 13mm · Weight: 6.3 grams
Mounting: .800 Silver · Period: Edwardian/Art Deco
Material: Shell (Sardonyx) · Carved in low relief

Greco-Roman Man Profiled Right Bar Pin/Brooch #1738
Size: 63mm x 16mm · Weight: 6.9 grams
Mounting: Gilt Bronze/Brass · Period: Victorian
Material: Hardstone · Carved in low relief

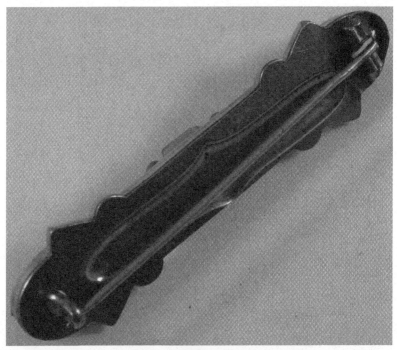

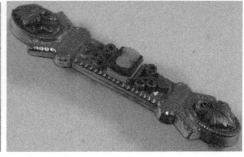

The contrasting color chain with attached cultured pearl is a contemporary addition to this piece. The chain is 14K gold-filled.

Greco-Roman Woman Profiled Left Brooch #1737
Size: 34mm x 27mm (Not Including Chain w/Pearl Pendant)
Weight: 5.7 grams
Mounting: Gilt Bronze/Brass · Period: Art Nouveau
Material: Hardstone · Carved in low relief

Buffalo Soldier Pendant #1723
Size: 45mm x 32mm
Weight: 18.2 grams
Mounting: Sterling Silver
Material: Hardstone (White Onyx)
Carved in medium relief
Period: Contemporary
(Special Commissioned)

Woman Profiled Left Pendant/Brooch #1647
Size: 29mm x 24mm · Weight: 5.6grams
Mounting: Gilt Bronze · Period: Art Deco
Material: Shell (Surrounded by Seed Pearls)

Scenic Brooch #1531
Size: 55mm x 47mm · Weight: 10.3 grams
Mounting: Gilt Brass · Period: Art Nouveau
Material: Shell

3 Graces Brooch #1685 · Size: 70mm x 55mm
Weight: 20.2 grams · Mounting: Gilt Bronze/Brass
Period: Early - Mid Victorian
Material: Shell (Carnelian) · Carved in low relief

The invention of the safety pin in 1849 was invaluable to Victorian jewelry-makers. To make the c-clasp more secure, a safety pin attached to a chain was often added to the mounting of cameos pieces.

Greco-Roman Woman Brooch
#1534
Size: 41mm x 33mm
Weight: 7.6 grams
Mounting: Gilt Brass/Bronze
Material: Shell
Period: Victorian

Habille Cameo - Woman Profiled Right #1391
Size: 46mm x 34mm · Weight: 11.1 grams · Approx. 3mm Diamond
Mounting: Not Mounted · Period: Art Deco
Material: Shell (Carnelian) · Carved in low relief

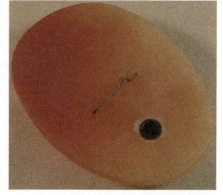

18" Greco-Roman Woman Necklace #1702
Brass Chain w/Faux Pearls
Size: Pendant-50mm x 37mm
Carved in low relief · Weight: 34.8 grams
Mounting: Brass
Period: Victorian/Art Nouveau

Victorian Woman Habille Pendant/Brooch #1421
with 3mm Faceted (Approx. 0.15 Carat) Diamond
Size: 58mm x 46mm · Weight: 17.7 grams
Mounting: Sterling · Period: Art Deco
Material: Shell (Carnelian)

Cherub/Putti Pendant #1417
Size: 44mm x 30mm · Weight: 15.7 grams
Mounting: Gilt Bronze · Period: Edwardian/Art Deco
Material: Hardstone (White Onyx) · Carved in medium relief

"Diana" the Moon Goddess Brooch #1403
Size: 31mm x 25mm · Weight: 4.5 grams
Mounting: Bronze · Period: Edwardian
Material: Shell (Carnelian) · Carved in low relief

"Mercury" Messenger for the Gods Pendant/Brooch #1719
Size: 28mm x 22mm · Weight: 4.3 grams · Mounting: .800 Silver
Period: Edwardian
Material: Shell (Sardonyx) · Carved in low relief

Greco-Roman Woman Brooch with Cherubs #1316
Size: 50mm x 47mm · Weight: 16.7 grams
Mounting: Heavily Gilded Brass · Period: Art Deco/Retro
Material: Shell · Carved in low relief

Woman Profiled Right Pendant/Brooch #1291
Size: 38mm x 30mm · Weight: 7.6 grams · Mounting: .900 Silver
Period: Edwardian
Material: Shell (Carnelian) · Carved in low relief

Victorian Sweetheart Couple Brooch #1725
Size: 56mm x 52mm · Weight: 20.9 grams · Mounting: Gilt Brass/Bronze
Period: Early - Mid Victorian
Material: Shell (Carnelian) · Carved in low relief

Woman Profiled Right Pendant/Brooch #1730
Size: 51mm x 42mm · Weight: 13.1 grams · Mounting: 10K Gold
Period: Mid - Late Victorian
Material: Shell (Carnelian) · Carved in low relief

Signed "GLP Co" (George L Paine Co) Pendant/Brooch #1727
Size: 37mm x 28mm · Weight: 6.0 grams · Mounting: 10K Gold
Period: Late Victorian - Early Edwardian
Material: Shell (Carnelian) · Carved in low relief

Mary with Baby Jesus and Sheppard's Pendant/Brooch #1718
Size: 45mm x 36mm · Weight: 11.5 grams · Mounting: Gilt Bronze
Period: Late Victorian - Early Edwardian
Material: Shell (Carnelian) · Carved in low relief

Woman Profiled Right Brooch #1323
Size: 50mm x 42mm
Weight: 9.9 grams
Mounting: Faux Tortoise Shell
Period: Art Nouveau
Material: Shell · Carved in low relief

Greco-Roman Woman Pendant/Brooch #1653
Size: 44mm x 34mm · Weight: 11.3 grams · Mounting: Gilt Bronze
Period: Edwardian
Material: Shell (Sardonyx) · Carved in low relief

Signed "Camexco & Co." Pendant/Brooch #1648
Size: 42mm x 33mm · Weight: 10.7 grams · Mounting: .800 Silver
Period: Art Deco/Retro
Material: Shell (Carnelian) · Carved in low relief

Woman Profiled Right Pendant/Brooch #1631
Size: 46mm x 34mm · Weight: 10.7 grams · Mounting: Gilt Bronze
Period: Early - Mid Victorian
Material: Shell (Carnelian) · Carved in low relief

"Artemis" Goddess of the Hunt Pendant/Brooch #1650
Size: 40mm x 32mm · Weight: 9.6 grams · Mounting: Gilt Sterling Silver
Period: Late Victorian - Early Edwardian
Material: Shell (Sardonyx) · Carved in low relief
Brooch is surrounded by natural seed pearls

This cameo spinner brooch/pendant swivels on an axis to reveal a glass enclosed compartment on the reverse side, probably to hold a lock of hair or a photo of a love one or a deceased relative.

"Bacchus" Wine God
Spinner Brooch/Pendant #1682
Size: 60mm x 53mm
Weight: 35.9 grams
Mounting: Gilt Bronze
Period: Early - Mid Victorian
Material: Shell (Carnelian)
Carved in low relief

Pastoral Scene Pendant/Brooch (missing pin) #1753
Size: 70mm x 60mm · Weight: 28.9 grams ·
Mounting: Pinchbeck/Gilt Brass · Period: Victorian
Material: Shell (Carnelian) · Carved in low relief

Woman Profiled Right Pendant/Brooch #1292 · Size: 37mm x 30mm
Weight: 6.8 grams · Mounting: Gilt Bronze
Period: Late Victorian - Mid Edwardian
Material: Shell (Carnelian) · Carved in low relief

Sioux Indian Woman Pendant #1525 · Size: 40mm x 34mm
Weight: 15.2 grams · Mounting: Gilt Bronze
Period: Contemporary (Special-Commissioned)
Material: Hardstone White Onyx carved in medium/high relief

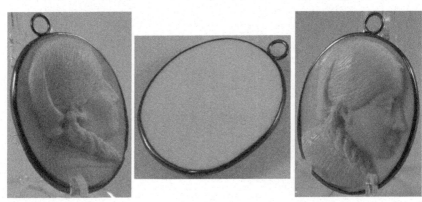

African-American Woman Pendant #1732
Size: 49mm x 41mm
Weight: 25.3 grams Mounting: Gilt Bronze
Period: Contemporary
Material: Hardstone (Amethyst & Chalcedony)
Carved in medium/high relief

Cameos depicting African-Americans are rare

Nez Perce Indian Pendant #1524
Size: 41mm x 30mm
Weight: 14.3 grams
Mounting: Gilt Bronze
Period: Contemporary
Material: Hardstone (Red Jasper)
Carved in medium/high relief

This special-commissioned cameo, that celebrate Native-Americans, was carved by an artisan who's ancestry as cameo carvers can be traced back to the 16th century and beyond.

Red Jasper is said to stimulate increased energy, strength and stamina.

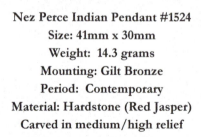

Moses Holding the Ten Commandments Pendant #1728
Size: 62mm x 44mm
Weight: 32.2 grams   Mounting: .900 Silver (stamped)
Period: Contemporary
Material: Hardstone (Agate) · Carved in high relief

This large and highly detailed cameo depicts Moses holding the Ten Commandments which are inscribed and readable in the Hebrew language. Moses was an early leader of the Hebrews and probably the most important figure in Judaism. He was raised in the court of the Pharaoh in Egypt, but then led the Hebrew people out of Egypt. Moses is said to have talked with God. His story is told in the Bible in the book of Exodus.

The select gemstone from which this cameo was carved, when held or exposed to daylight, has a bluish hue.

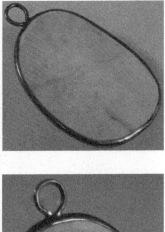

The difficulty of carving a stone cameo in extremely high relief, as this extraordinary cameo is carved, makes this a truly rare find.

"Apollon" Hellenistic God (with lyre) Pendant #1521 · Size: 48mm x 37mm
Weight: 25.6 grams Mounting: Gilt Bronze
Period: Believed to be a Late Victorian - Early Edwardian cameo that was mounted or remounted in a later period
Material: Hardstone (White Onyx) · Carved in extremely high relief

Greco-Roman Woman Profiled Right Brooch #1530
Size: 22mm x 22mm · Weight: 3 grams
Mounting: 10K Gold · Period: Art Nouveau
Material: Shell · Carved in low/medium relief

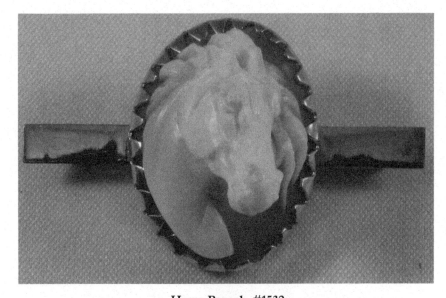

Horse Brooch #1532
Size: 23mm x 18mm x 37mm · Weight: 4.8 grams

Mounting: 10K Gold
Period: Art Deco
Material: Shell (Carnelian)
Carved in high relief

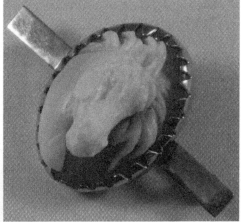

Michelangelo's Pieta Image #1593
Size: 60mm x 44mm · Weight: 17.1 grams
Mounting: Not Mounted · Period: Unknown
Material: Shell (Carnelian) · Carved in low relief

Roman Goddess Chariot Cameo #1747
Size: 50mm x 39mm · Weight: 9 grams
Mounting: Not Mounted
Period: Contemporary
Material: Shell (Sardonyx) ·Carved in low relief

Roman Soldier & Woman #1610
Size: 48mm x 37mm · Weight: 10 grams
Mounting: Not Mounted · Period: Unknown
Material: Shell · Carved in low relief

Woman Profiled Right Brooch #1507
Size: 27mm x 25mm · Weight: 4.3 grams · Mounting: Gilt Brass/Bronze
Period: Mid Victorian · Material: Shell (Sardonyx) · Carved in low relief

Greco-Roman Woman Pendant #1375 Size: 39mm x 30mm
Weight: 14.6 grams Mounting: Gilt Bronze
Period: Believed to be an early Edwardian cameo
Material: Hardstone (White Onyx) · Carved in high relief
Hair has been color enhanced

Image believed to be that of Faustina the Younger, daughter of Roman Emperor Antoninus Pius and Roman Empress Faustina the Elder

Angel & Woman #1609
Size: 44mm x 34mm · Weight: 6.3 grams
Mounting: Not Mounted · Period: Unknown
Material: Shell (Carnelian) · Carved in low relief

Greco-Roman Woman Profiled Right
Brooch #1752
Size: 48mm x 40mm
Weight: 10.9 grams
Mounting: Rolled Gold
Period: Mid - Late Victorian
Material: Shell (Sardonyx)
Carved in low relief

Cameo Rings and Stickpins

Stick pins are very often confused with hat pins. Although their overall design is similar, stick pins are not as long as hat pins and generally have more elaborately decorated tops. It is not unusual to find stick pins embedded with precious stones and made of precious metals. Upper-class Englishmen of the 18th century originally wore stick pins to secure the folds of a cravat, a short, wide strip of fabric worn by men around the neck and tucked inside an open-necked shirt, a modern-day equivalent of a necktie. In the 19th century, the wearing of a stick pin became as popular with women as with men. Today, a stick pin can add a touch of elegance when worn on the lapel of a man's or woman's jacket, or accent a necktie or scarf.

Greco-Roman Image Ring #1742 · Size: 6
Weight: 2.1 grams · Mounting: 14K Gold
Period: Victorian
Material: Hardstone (Agate) · Carved in medium relief

Greco-Roman Image Ring #1714
Size: 6 · Cameo Size: 16mm x 12mm
Weight: 6.3 grams · Mounting: 10K Gold
Period: Art Deco/Retro
Material: Hardstone (Agate)
Carved in low relief

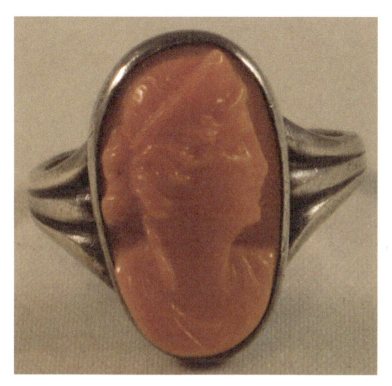

Greco-Roman Woman Image Ring #1430
Size: 6.5 · Cameo Size: 16mm x 10mm
Weight: 4.1 grams · Mounting: Sterling
Period: Victorian Material: Coral (Salmon)
Carved in medium/high relief

Greco-Roman Image Ring #1422
Size: 6 · Cameo Size: 29mm x 24mm · Weight: 10 grams
Mounting: .800 Silver
Period: Edwardian
Material: Hardstone · Carved in medium relief

Greco-Roman Image Ring #1705
Size: 5.5 · Cameo Size: 21mm x 12mm · Weight: 4.3 grams
Mounting: 18K White Gold
Period: Art Deco
Material: Hardstone · Carved in medium relief

Greco-Roman Image Ring #1715
Size: 5.5 · Weight: 3.2 grams
Mounting: 10K Yellow Gold
Period: Late Victorian - Mid Edwardian
Material: Hardstone · Carved in low - medium relief

Greco-Roman Image Ring #1713
Size: 11 · Weight: 6.4 grams
Mounting: Sterling Silver
Period: Mid Victorian - Early Edwardian
Material: Hardstone · Carved in low relief

Greco-Roman Image Ring #1721
Size: 5 · Cameo Size: 12mm x 14mm · Weight: 5.8 grams
Mounting: 18K White Gold
Period: Art Deco
Material: Amethyst Stone · Carved in low relief

Wedgewood Ring #1707
Size: 6 · Cameo Size: 18mm x 8mm · Weight: 2.6 grams
Mounting: Sterling
Period: Unknown · Material: Green Jasper

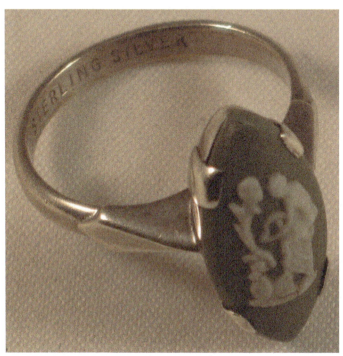

Roman Soldier Image Intaglio Ring #1701
Size: 6.5 · Weight: 1.8 grams
Mounting: 9K Gold
Period: Victorian · Material: Hardstone (Black

Roman Soldier Image Ring #1739
Size: 7 · Weight: 5.4 grams
Mounting: 14K White Gold
Period: Art Deco
Material: Hardstone (Black Onyx)

Stick Pin #1515
Size: 13mm x 16mm x 47mm
Weight: 1.5 grams
Mounting: Gilt Brass/Bronze
Period: Victorian/Edwardian
Material: Shell (Carnelian)

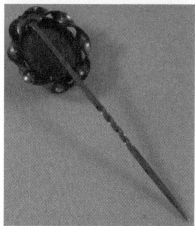

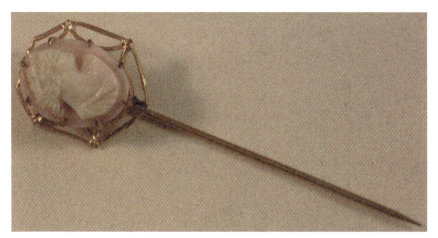

Woman Profiled Right Stick Pin #1487 · Size: 15mm x 20mm x 63mm
Weight: 3.4 grams Mounting: Gilt Brass
Period: Victorian/Edwardian
Material: Shell (Angel Skin)

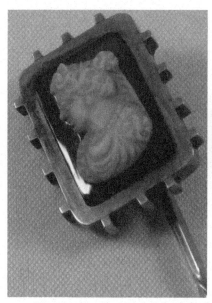
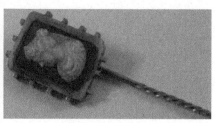

Woman Profiled Left Stick Pin #1448 · Size: 21mm x 16mm x 72mm
Weight: 4.1 grams Mounting: Gilt Brass
Period: Victorian/Edwardian
Material: Hardstone

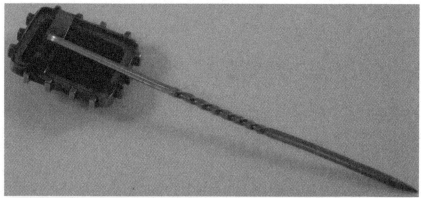
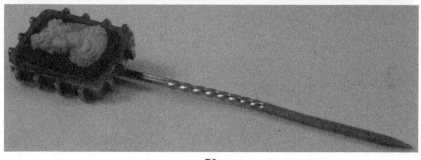

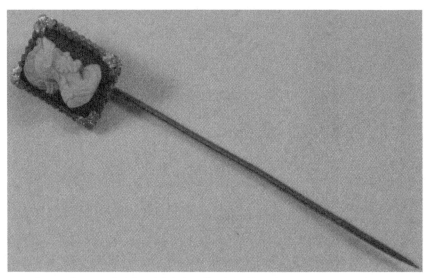

Greco-Roman Soldier Stick Pin #1538 · Size: 18mm x 14mm x 80mm
Weight: 4.9 grams Mounting: 10K Gold
Period: Victorian/Edwardian
Material: Hardstone

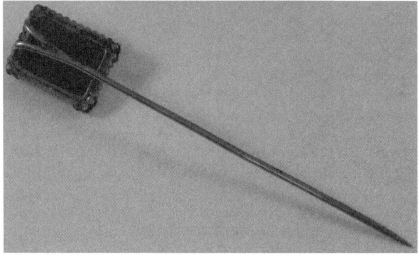

Cameos Made From Bakelite and Alternative Materials

The Art Deco period ushered in the use of Bakelite in costume jewelry-making. Dr. Leo Baekeland invented Bakelite in the early 1900s and patented his discovery in 1909. Bakelite's heat resistance, strength and its ability to be molded and carved made it ideal for use in a number of applications including jewelry-making. Bakelite's use in producing affordable jewelry reached its peak between the 1930s and 40s. Quality pieces were sold in high-end stores like Saks Fifth Avenue as well as in Woolworth's and Sears.

Jasperware is a type of pottery/stoneware developed by Josiah Wedgwood in the 1770s. Wedgwood Jasperware cameos have dating clues stamped on the reverse of the images. Prior to 1860, you will only find the word "Wedgwood" and possibly a single letter and/or potter's mark; from 1860 to 1891 there was a three letter stamping system used indicating, in order, the month, potter and year. The third letter in the series correspond with the following years:

O-1860 P-1861 Q-1962 R-1863 S-1864 T-1865 U-1866 V-1867 W-1868 X-1869 Y-1870 Z-1871 A-1872 B-1873 C-1874 D-1875 E-1876 F-1877 G-1878 H-1879 I-1880 J-1881 K-1882 L-1883 M-1884 N-1885 (Starting in 1886 and until 1897 the first characters in the dating system were re-used) O-1886 P-1887 Q-1888 R-1889 S-1890.

The "WEDGWOOD" and "ENGLAND" stamps will appear with the letter starting in 1891; T– 1891 U-1892 V-1893 W-1894 X-1895 Y-1896 Z-1897 A-1898 B-1899 C-1900 D-1901 E-1902 F-1903 G-1904 H-1905 I-1906 J-1907.

The "WEDGWOOD" and "MADE IN ENGLAND" stamps will appear with the letter starting in 1908-1969; from 1970 to the present a single stamp "WEDGWOOD MADE IN ENGLAND" will appear on the piece.

Wedgwood Brooch & Screw-Back Earrings #1529
Size: Brooch-53mm x 41mm, Earrings-27mm x 19mm
Weight: 20.0 grams Mounting: Sterling Silver
Period: Victorian · Material: Blue Jasper

Wedgwood Brooch/Pendant & Locking Shepherd's Hook Earrings #1499
Size: Brooch-31mm x 31mm, Earrings-22mm x 22mm
Weight: Brooch-7.2 grams, Earrings-6.5 grams Mounting: Brass
Period: Contemporary (1966-1968) · Material: Green Jasper

Putti Playing Music Brooch #1586 · Size: 46mm x 46mm
Weight: 18.7 grams Mounting: .800 Silver
Period: Victorian · Material: Bisque Porcelain

Cameo Clamper Bracelet & Brooch Set #1698
Size: 67mm x 67mm (Brooch) · Weight: 30.1 grams (Brooch)
Size: 47mm Wide (Bracelet) · Weight: 60.3 grams (Bracelet)
Material: Celluloid Cameo · Balance of Materials Bakelite
Period: Retro · Material: Silver

Black Bakelite often fail the simichrome test (as this did). I never recommend using the hot needle test when alternate methods are available. The hot needle test was used to confirm this piece.

Woman Profiled Right Brooch #1736 · Size: 60mm x 49mm
Weight: 21.5 grams · Mounting: Wood
Period: Art Deco/Retro · Material: Resin

Woman Profiled Right Brooch #1579 · Size: 48mm x 42mm
Weight: 15.9 grams Mounting: Gold-plated Metal
Period: Art Nouveau · Material: Dublet Black Glass & Celluloid Cameo
with 4 Black Faceted Stones

Victorian Woman Brooch #1729 · Size: 62mm x 54mm
Weight: 19.3 grams · Mounting: Vulcanite/Bog Oak (Bottom Layer)
Period: Victorian · Material: Whitby Jet Cameo Image
The central panel is highly polished carved Whitby Jet
Pin support appears to have been replaced

Vulcanite, made by combining and heating the sap of the Euphorbia or Ficus trees from Malaysia with sulfur, is more often molded rather than carved. Jet and Bog Oak are fossilized woods. Bog Oak, found in Ireland, has a black or very dark brown color. Whitby Jet, found in Whitby, England, has a shiny black color, but could also have a matte finish. Unlike Vulcanite, Bog Oak and Jet are always carved rather than molded.

**Woman Profiled Right Pendant #1726 · Size: 66mm x 40mm
Weight: 31.1 grams Mounting: Sterling
Period: Art Deco
Material: Doublet Resin Cameo mounted to Black Glass**

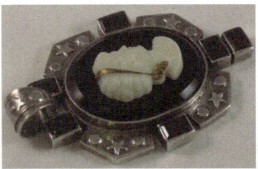

Woman Profiled Right Brooch #1745
Size: 56mm x 47mm · Weight: 23.2 grams
Mounting: Rootbeer Bakelite
with Brass Accents
Period: Late Art Deco/ Early Retro
Material: Applied Resin Cameo

Woman Profiled Left Brooch #1746 · Size: 46mm x 39mm
Weight: 14.8 grams · Mounting: Brass · Period: Late Art Deco/Early Retro
Material: Bakelite (Cherry Amber and Black)

Woman Profiled Right Brooch #1743 · Size: 39mm x 31mm
Weight: 14.7 grams Mounting: Brass
Period: Art Deco · Material: Pink Glass
Probably made to imitate angel skin coral

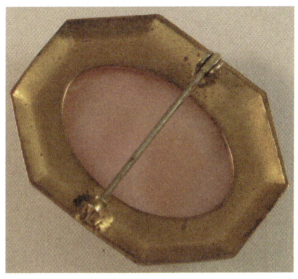

Mourning Brooch/Locket #1567 · Size: 48mm x 48mm
Weight: 37.2 grams Mounting: Brass
Period: Art Nouveau/Art Deco
Material: Doublet (Resin Cameo and Black Glass)

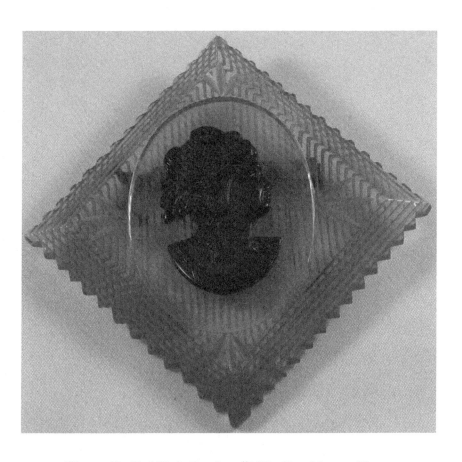

Woman Profiled Right Pendant #1693 · Size: 56mm x 56mm
Weight: 28.6 grams Mounting: Apple Juice Bakelite
Period: Late Art Deco/Early Retro
Material: Applied Celluloid Black Cameo Image

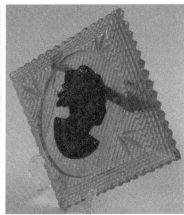

Woman Profiled Right Brooch #1234 · Size: 70mm x 57mm
Weight: 62.6 grams Mounting: Gilt Bronze/Brass
Period: Art Deco · Material: Celluloid

Woman Profiled Left Brooch #1688 · Size: 80mm x 30mm
Weight: 13.3 grams Mounting: Bronze
Period: Art Deco · Material: Celluloid Cameo & Black Faceted Stones

Victorian Woman Brooch #1654 · Size: 58mm x 45mm
Weight: 11.7 grams Mounting: Sterling (Front) & Metal (Back)
Period: Art Nouveau/Art Deco· Material: Sterling Silver
Attributed to Thomas F. Brogan, NY (1896-1930)

"Minerva" Brooch #1605 · Size: 37mm x 37mm
Weight: 10.2 grams Mounting: Bronze
Period: Mid - Late Victorian · Material: Pressed Horn

Horn is a natural plastic made from the horns and tusks of animals. Pictured is a beautiful example from the Victorian period. The horn is ground, pressed, heated and dyed to produce truly eye-catching pieces of jewelry.

"Mercury" Messenger for the Gods Brooch #1411 · Size: 73mm x 54mm
Weight: 20.0 grams Mounting: Gold-tone Stamped Metal
Period: Art Deco/Retro · Material: Dark Red and Clear Paste Stones

Woman Profiled Right Pendant #1341 · Size: 54mm x 45mm
Signed "Whiting & Davis Co."
17 Jewels M6 Caravelle Watch in Working Condition on Reverse Side
Weight: 51.0 grams Mounting: Gilt Bronze/Brass
Period: Retro · Material: Celluloid

Native American Pendant/Brooch #1389 · Size: 54mm x 34mm
Note that pin is missing · Designer: Carolyn Pollack
Weight: 23.1 grams Mounting: Sterling Silver
Period: Contemporary · Material: Resin

CPSIA information can be obtained
at www.ICGtesting.com
Printed in the USA
BVOW05s1739211217
503320BV00016BA/721/P